Pieces of Me

Elizabeth Ramirez

BookLeaf Publishing

India | USA | UK

Presentation by *BookLeaf Publishing*

Web: www.bookleafpub.com

E-mail: info@bookleafpub.com

ISBN : 9789357447775

First edition 2021

DEDICATION

This book is dedicated to love and fate. Thank you, Universe.

ACKNOWLEDGEMENT

I would like to acknowledge Book Leaf Publishing for making my dream a reality. Thank you for this opportunity to share my words with the world and reach others with my writing.

PREFACE

This book is for everyone. I hope the words jump off the page and speak to you, reader.

First Summer

My first summer was breathtaking. The swelter of the heat took me by surprise, grabbing me and pulling me towards the rays of its sun. I lie still in the passion, while it's warmth overtook my entirety. My first summer swept me off my feet and lead me into an ocean I'd never dive into, head first. The water, at first touch ran cold and my body could barely navigate its depth. The comfort crept up from my toes, moving through each inch of me, mellowing my heart to a steady beat. My first summer was so intricately beautiful. It was mysterious and numbing. Free yet caging. Brutal yet honest. My first summer let it's fervor engulf me. My first summer was absolutely unforgettable. I basked in its gaudiness. My first summer rocked me sound asleep with promises of a brighter sun. Endow me with your sun, first summer. But first, summer. Watch me walk into you without fear. I am not afraid of your scorching fingertips touching each inch of my body. You're grabbing onto me so tight. Hold onto me, first summer. Your rays surround me, first summer. I feel your aura first lover. I'm forever bound to that, first summer.

Let Me In

Apply tension to the pressure point of no return and we'll break in regression. The lack of self-love haunts me and you're possessed with reasonable doubt. Mindless me, exonerating you for all the things you overthought about. But I do. forgive. For, give and take. I give you my all and you take me further into your vulnerability. But moments of inconsistency impeded the circulation of our energies, we became disconnected. I feel you spiritually. I exist in your existentialism. All you have to do is trust, fall into me. So deep inside, the darkness fades to make way for the sun that will grow inside of me. Our bodies entwined with the branches on the Tree of Life. We disentangle the confusion and begin to unravel this mysterious love. Experiencing the rush when both our fingertips touch the glass. Although it cuts deep, let me undress your wounds, carefully, intently and slowly so I can gauge the severity of your pain. I can take it, the heaviness of the weight you carried when you first roamed this Universe. Lost and found me in the darkest depths of space. Screaming in silence. You lulled me with

your enrapturing words of enlightened love, I'm
holding on too.

Dear Reader

When did life start to turn around like this? My hope is sinking and now I'm drowning in this filth weighing me down. Everything around me is still, only my fingers quiver in the vastness. I am hurting for you, them and us all at once. I needed you to show me how to brave danger. Instead I learned to cower in fear and walk with my head down. I was your first burden and both our minds are overrun with demons of decisions made and opportunities lost. I want to right your wrongs, but now I am busy writing mine. These emotions overwhelm me, I cannot stay afloat so with this ocean I've cried, there's only room to sink. I drown in your lies and those promises were empty like the look in your eyes when I realized I've died this way in your mind time and time again. Still, I find myself through losing you.

Every Trip

I traverse from the inside of your brain to the outside of your mind. Head to toe. Took a left, right across your soul. Straight up your spine until I reside in your temporal lobe. I dreamt you into my reality. My thoughts run wild because with you I'm uncaged. I am the wind wisping through the willow tree, whispering to your spirit. You strip me of my worry and redress me with your fearlessness. Your strength is addicting, a life line I inhale eagerly. I'm so high up in the clouds, coming down would indefinitely paralyze me. The fog is thick when you enter me. But when we take off, everything goes, smoothly. Your breath is turbulent on my skin, nonetheless I breathe you in. Effortlessly, you navigate my plains. You speak to my land as if you traveled her once before. But you've only been here once, I would have recognized you. I would have seen your face in the brush of leaves that surrounded my vision. You are unfamiliar to me, like cold air kissing me when my first summer ends. I adapt to you and follow you into this new place we landed in.

Ode to Self

You were waiting for me to come and save you, but I was so preoccupied that I never showed up. I never saw potential in you, always doubted you. Even good enough was never enough. You masked all of your pain with everything you wanted to be and everything you knew you couldn't. You sat alone and cried wishing you could escape all the fears you needed to face. I cut you a thousand times and relished in the sting as your tears washed away the blood. I am the voice you hear screaming to get out. Just let me out, into a world where I'm seen. The real you. The world isn't blind to your beauty as you are, Self. Hello, there dumb girl. You never could listen because you've never truly seen. No sound when you cry out. I'm screaming for you to save yourself, sweet girl.

Caged

These societal chains link back to the roots of evil. You held me down, hands wrapped so gracefully around my neck. I gasped for life as my breath slowly escaped me. You let go just in time to allow my mind to survive but when you were ready, you smothered me again. Together we dance across hot stones, but you enjoy the blaze. You rejoice in my struggle to walk on. You punish me in the worst way, locking me into my mind while the key to release is hidden. So I'm stuck here in your dungeon of misery, the master suite of your despair. Still I visit when I am free, intrigued by your wildness. Enticed by your danger. I feel powerful in the routine we have created as I get to know you, cage.

Weight

The heaviness in your mind was hard to navigate in the dark. Still I could see shadows through the cold, thick black. The fog surrounding me blurred the ideas you'd thought you formed. I came in feeling the walls of your mind, inch by inch. Your thoughts were rough and so my fingers became calloused and began to bleed as I clawed away at your intensity. I'm here at the forefront of your emotional door, let me in. On my shoulders I'm carrying baggage that may seem light for you. Your door is ajar, the opening not yet wide enough to submerse myself in your home so for the night I'll take shelter in your damage.

Bad Dream

Nightmares haunt my sleep. Subconscious thoughts terrorize my free will to dream. I lay still and try my hardest to fight the heaviness that sneaks into my eyes. Eventually sleep overtakes me and I drift into an intergalactic world where anything goes. All of my fears stand upright in front of me daring me to be brave. I cringe. Wake up, I say. I cannot awake because I am not asleep. Realities blur like the curvature of her body and my sexuality, as I fantasize her every move. Encapsulate me, then take me in the form I am, vehemently. I see familiar faces in the thick. An abusive father, a lifeless mother. Why is life less, mother? Why this camera put here, continually rolling, capturing my pain and replaying it all in real time, slow motion.

Hello, Love.

When you meet her, she will be breathtaking. She will have eyes that speak words of pain and desire. Her passion radiates off of her as she coils up underneath you on that cold Winter morning. You tighten your grip on her body as you begin to speak in tongues. Can you taste me lover? My river is ever flowing. Swim inside me and feel me as I rock your boat. My waves crash into you as you dip in and out of my reservoir. Go deeper, my winds whisper as I begin to delicately submerge you. Come into me. I indulge in your creamed caramel skin. My taste buds pop with sparks of your essence. Essential to the whole experience. Hands down, never have I ever experienced this.

Warning Signs

I walked the universe wildly, penetrated by the unfamiliar. The burning ash from the volcanos danced on my cheeks, stinging me gracefully. I enjoy your pain because I will soon reap your healing. Soporific lies had your audience unimpressed. I allow you to inculcate me with your destructive view. Infiltrating me with your ideas of something more. A butterfly passes, it's wings fragile from your zephyr. My breath flutters. I read the signs, the lights flash brightly in my eyes, five hundred feet away from your soul. I'll go the distance. I reach my destination and you are back at the starting point of where we left off.

Thank you, Danger.

I met you in a dark place. I was cold and in need of the warmth of love. I fell in love with the mask you wore and the masquerade you played. You take hold of me and now I am nothing but weight on your shoulders. We're moving too fast, I can't catch my breath. You pace through the thickness of the air. Back and forth with your words and I resent you and your officious behavior. Now we're high off the possibilities and what could've been. I stay up with you all night, sleepless. Helpless to your persuasion. You ignite the gas light to my insecurity. Remind me of all you do so that all I am left with is the dependence. I release you back to the dark place you are in.

Poem 12

This piece shall be like no other. I allow my thoughts to come freely and I let my soul guide my fingers. I begin to write from that place in my brain where the thoughts scream and the trauma hushes the doubt. I am free in this moment where I don't think. I write and I'm right when I tell my story because it is mine. Too late to right wrongs when you turn to me and shit goes left. I am a raconteur who is simply allowing you to feel my nouns and adjectives in real time. Fear crashes into me like waves on the sandy beaches I daydream about drowning in. Let my art form take over you. Lets these words dance in your mind when you look to solitude from the background noise. Hear me. I need you to listen closely to the silent burden I carry. Watch me jump off the page and slip into something more unique.

Rooted

Envy burns in your eyes. I can't withstand your roaring flame so I shield myself from your embers. The crackling of the fire is louder than the branches being snapped off the Sequoia that feeds your blaze. You've injured this shrub and it will be generations before it can sprout something durable enough to protect from your next cut, but the forest of my pain supplies you with endless wood. You wished for my seed to die so I would not grow, yet I flourished. My branches grew thicker and my leaves blossomed with vivid colors. I stumped you each time you hacked away at my trunk. Now stronger than ever, I am growing wonderfully. The sun shines down on my thick skin and I bask in its energy.

Thy Father

I don't know any part of you. We didn't have time to belong to each other. Do you feel connected with me? That connection that connects the dots and makes us make sense? I am half of you. I dream a dream where we are familiar. You are from the sky. You are the wind sweeping past me and the stars I wish on. The universe seems to roam with me hand in hand, is that you Father? Will we be reunited in another lifetime? I protect myself with all I know myself to be. I scream at the moon and pray the vibration reaches you.

Rush

Thank you for changing my life, sweet. You love me in a way that I needed from the start and unaware of your power, I fell for you. Adrenaline rushed through my veins as you came into me. Overpowered my entirety and became mine entirely. You don't mind the inconsistencies that come with me and all that I cannot consistently be. Let this rush surge through us. I learn where I go wrong as we bump into the rails and our bodies shake. But carelessly we could care less. We're together and that's all we see and feel.

Hunt for the Moon

I follow the illumination reflecting off the ground. While the stars dance in the murky sky, I sprint through the fields. The thistle cuts away at my body, left bare but I endure the pain. It is Fear herself I am running from. I smell her through the tall grass that hides her shadow. She tastes me on her tongue, traces of white wine still dancing on her taste buds. "Face me" she roars into the wind, the vibration of her rumble slowing me down. I lose balance. Why could I not see that I was attracted to her risk? Her touch sent electricity through my veins, igniting this spark inside me that made me want to overpower her. I meet her every night in my dreams. She incessantly scolds me, reminds me how weak I've been. Only to leave me the next day to face her yet again. Should I be running beside you, Fear? Shall I let that unfamiliar light guide us with its surrounding clouds of blue-green? Am I seeing clearly or is your fog clouding my vision? I fight myself for the truth of your beauty. When I needed to face you, all I could see was myself. There I reflect, stuck

inside the mirror of the impure authentic self I
want to be.

Oak Tree

Your mind is ravished by your impure thoughts while your soul is ravenous for the greatness that lies within you. A hunger pang soothed by your strength. You speak kind words into existence even through the resistance of the pain that exists inside of you. Deeply rooted my dear Oak Tree. Your ripples tell stories of past lives only the paper from your bark can handle so I read between your lines. Your words jump off the page and I hear your cries through each syllable my mouth will allow me to articulate. You are wise, Oak Tree. I climb you with the determination it took the earth to plant your seed in the perfect cool, wet soil. The rain waters you so perfectly, no drought shall ever fall on you. You are growing beautifully, Oak Tree. Your heartwood, although passed with the spirit that held you, is growing wonderfully. Your layers go on for cosmic centuries and hold secrets only the Universe and I can know. I have arrived at your core, Oak Tree.

Grand Rising, Self.

I woke up this morning. Mind clear, eyes open. I faced the demons that will haunt my soul again in the next life. I've paid my karmic debt and now I walk in hand with my strength. I have never seen myself in this light. Bright enough to show me the way. Is this what it feels like to love, Self? I wish on a dandelion and watch as its soft feathery petals carry my dreams into the Universe. It was so hard to see your beauty Self, but now you are glowing.

Full Moon

We stayed awake talking under the full moon. You intrigued me with your kaleidoscope of dreams. Reflected all of my imperfect patterns. Your deep baritone welcomed me to stay. Your touch was electric. You saw me. For me, it was mesmerizing. But our souls were in retrograde. Rewinding effort put forth into our fifth dimension. I am awake searching the sky for the stars. We count the clouds together and imagine lying our heads on their fluffy pillows. The sky takes away our fears. The gravity brings us back to Earth. We study our full moon and learn its every feature. I dance under this moon with you and we bask in the riptides from is magnetic energy.

Waves

You let your fingers do the talking as your hands enunciate my curves. I look in your eyes and I see through you. We kiss and our tongues dance as if they've practiced a thousand times. Here we are free, at our beach. Our oceans flow swiftly yet rough, but we know these seas. My water is warm when you step in and you feel how wet I can be. You're wrapped inside my body. I hold you tight. You swim inside me with a perfect pace. Keep going until you reach the point of no return. Where can you go after you've came into me? Deeper. What are you looking for inside me, lover? When you step out, you lie down in my soft sands. Each granule adding its own significant part to why you love it here so much. I wrap myself around you. The cold air comes, unexpectedly so we adjust our bodies and use our sultriness to keep each other warm.

21 Pieces

I found myself in twenty-one pieces. Not fully shattered but each piece having it's own significant groove to explain its story. As you ran each individual finger across, you realized I was more than just a tainted piece of glass. I was unique. My dark pieces moved you and the light reflecting from me gave hope that I would be able to be fixed. You found me, in twenty-one pieces.